i am
A Poetic Journey Towards Self Definition

By: Stephanie M. Pruitt
Keisha D. Rucker, Editor

Infotainment Talent and Publishing
Nashville, TN 2002

© Copyright 2002

All rights reserved.
No part of this book may be reproduced or utilized in any form without permission from the publisher. Inquiries should be addressed to:
**Infotainment Talent and Publishing
1708 21st Avenue South, Suite #149
Nashville, TN 37212**

First Edition
ISBN 0-9723114-0-8

Front cover photo by Carlton Wilkinson
ArtWorks Studio
Nashville, TN
artwrksitg@aol.com

Design by 3RD Room Studio
Shannon Jenkins
Nashville, TN
www.3rdroomstudio.com

Back cover headshot by Myra Harding
Memories By Myra
Nashville, TN

For Nia, Christy, Brendalyn and Stephen.

I am a better person
because of the love we share.

"If you know my poetry, you know me"
— Anonymous

table of contents

I AM 7–11
    I AM 8-11

I AM Who You Perceive Me to Be 13–33
    Contrived Reality 14-17
    Afro Dreams 18-19
    Hymn #605 20-21
    His and Hers Haikus 22
    For Mammy and Mrs 23-24
    In The Dark 25
    Little Black Girl 26-27
    Poetry 28-30
    They Too Will Fall 31
    Weapon of Mass Instruction 32

I AM Half of a Relationship 35–52
    Blind Faith 36-37
    Marvel of the Black Man 38-39
    Untitled and Unlimited 40
    Realizations 41
    Postpartum 42-44
    Reason 45
    Silence 46-47
    Together 48
    Unity 49
    Little Sister 50
    Mama's Opus 51-52

I AM What I Experience 53-70
    Memories of Ecstasy 54-55
    Monotone 56-57
    Mechanically 58
    Rhythm 59-60
    Quilting 61-63
    History Whostory 64
    Your Presence or Absence 65-66
    I Saw a Man Cry 67
    Morning Drink......................... 68
    Just Dessert 69-70

I AM My Thoughts 71-91
    Evolution 72
    The Self in Me...................... 73-74
    Stuttering Strength.................. 75-77
    For Us By Us....................... 78-81
    Choice Words......................... 82
    For Sisters Sonia and Nikki 83
    Understanding Maslowe 84
    Headlines............................ 85
    Creationism 86
    Peace Like a River 87-91

Letter From the Author 92-93

Acknowledgements 94

i am

"Do not wish to be anything but what you are,
and to be that perfectly."
— St. Francis De Sales

i am

I AM going to tell you who I AM
I AM going to tell you who I AM just as soon as I know who
I AM
Because sometimes I AM confused and have
to wonder who I AM
I AM a little unsure of myself these days
Because my thoughts are caught in a maze
I AM strong but must have some mental muscle cramps
Because I AM not so amped about myself
I AM reading all these books that make me take a look inside and
Now I can't hide from the light I AM finding and
unwinding into something recognizable
I AM filtering through old and new stimuli
I AM living in truth, which hurts but not
quite as much as the lie
I AM facing this mirror that is pretty ugly
I AM not going to turn away
Hey say I AM looking for a fix
Can you give me a hit
The walls are closing in so I AM
Moving towards the center which is not a bad place to be because it
is easier to balance in the center and I AM in need of

some balance
I AM holding my arms out wide to keep the forces from
pushing me to one side and I AM winning but to win you
have to lose something
Opportunity costs they call it and
I AM paying
I AM caught up with that bill which has
bent my will so far down that I saw my shadow through
my legs
I AM catching my breath
'Cause I need it to live
Inhale exhale inhale
exhale inhale ex
ex ex extracurricular activities
extramarital affairs
extraterrestrial visions
extraordinary amounts of pressure
I AM breathing and breathing
and breathing the stank air of pollution
Clouding my mind
Might as well smoke
I AM quitting bad habits though
so that ain't really an option
I AM breathing and breathing and breathing
with nostrils flared like I AM about to fight because I AM
I AM breathing to fight my self
To fight the urge

To fight the surge
To fight the verge of collapse
I AM
I AM
I AM probably sounding a bit crazy to you right now
But I don't have the energy to think about your thoughts
I AM thinking mine
I AM standing up for me
I AM not going to sit down or back for you
I AM breathing easier now you know
Let air flow I AM
I AM stepping away from the edge
Pledge allegiance to the I AM in me
It's there you know
Divinity
I AM divine
It's taken a lot of time
Had to unwind what was tightly wrapped
I AM loving what is here to love which
is a lot
I AM a lot
Others may look back and leave a salty spot on the
ground but
I AM traveling never to regret
Never to fondly reminisce to the point I wish for another
Time
I AM here now

How can I be anywhere else
I AM that I AM
From beginning to end I
Am
From light to
dark
to light again
I AM
Every single 1-2-3-hundred and sixty degrees whole I
AM
I AM moving but not revolving
I AM evolving
Moving into places I have never been
or can't remember
I AM clean
So fresh and so clean
Clean
I AM I
Am I
Am
Am I?
I AM!

[i̇.AM.]

i am who you perceive me to be

"Examine the labels you apply to yourself.
Every label is a boundary or limit you will not allow yourself to cross."
– Dwayne Dyer

contrived reality

Is it my
Blood or behavior
Color or culture
Pigmentation or personality
That makes me black
Now, I know
whether I'm
Charcoal or chocolate
Honey or hickory
Caramel or copper
Cinnamon or Sudanian dark brown
I AM still black
It is not the same however
when you look at how I act
Do I listen to Busta Rhymes or Bach
Am I twenty minutes late or right on the clock
Are the ends of my words cut off
or do I speak with perfect diction
All this makes me wonder
if my reality is based out of fact or fiction
Before you shrug this off
as a personal psychosocial issue
I must work through
Take a moment to look at yourself
Who or what are you

I AM Who You Perceive Me to Be

Can you be defined by the color of your skin
Or would you rather people see what lies within
And if you look beyond your shade or hue
Do you actually know how to define you
If we were all color blind
Would we still live
in the same state of mind
And while we're on the subject
who classified me anyway
Am I black because that's what other people see
Or is it because of the blood,
love and history that runs through me
But wait
Don't misconstrue
my words
I love who I AM
Mocha brown skin and all
I mean
You can look at me
and see
that I AM Divine
And it's not that I AM full of myself
But then again
whom else would I be filled with
Besides my Maker who permeates
the deepest caverns of my being
You see my divinity

is not connected to any physical trait
Can you relate
My divinity's foundation
is not something
you can physically see
Are you still with me
My divinity
comes from my Spirit,
which is a manifestation of God
And as we know
Spirits,
which have no body,
have no color
So really
Can I be summed up
by words like
black,
colored,
afro….I'm sorry,
African American,
negro, nigra
Well,
I guess I can be called black now
Because I'm talking this "black stuff" talk
But what if you
one day hear me say
that affirmative action is not the way

Then my black card will be revoked
And I'm nothing but a sell out who don't know her folk
On the other hand if you see me
walking down the street
with my dread locks twisted tight
or head wrap wrapped right
It doesn't matter what's actually in my mind
You'll think
yeah, she's black all right
What I'm trying to get at is a very simple notion
All these social constructs we depend upon
really aren't worth the commotion
Because when you look at me
There is only one thing you can truly see
It should be clear to you that because of my creator
I AM divine
Divinity is in our nature.

[i̇ₐₘ]

afro dreams

I've been walking around seeing
Afro dreams
and
Dread loc visions
And that is beautiful to me
We want to look in the mirror
see ourselves
and say
REVOLUTIONARY
That is me!

I've been walking around seeing
Afro dreams
and
Dread loc visions
With bodies draped in dashikis
We want to be able to write in big black words
on the front of our
autobiographies
REVOLUTIONARY
That is me!

Yes
I have been seeing
Afro dreams

and
Dread loc visions
but do not mistake people of
these
Visions
as Visionaries
Because
Hairstyles and clothes
Don't mean the person
Knows
What's really going on

hymn #605

Nobody saw her step down the aisle and sneak into a sliver of a seat on the new velvet pew. While the congregation sang with their chins toward God, her long neck was buried deep in the curved shoulders that spoke of defeat.

Nobody saw her massage her own aching hand, when the song leader said turn to hymn number 605. Children played with the tattered string bookmark while her fingers traced the thin page. She didn't even realize she was crying until she tasted the salty wetness with each word. "Just as I AM and waiting not, to rid my soul of one dark blot."

Nobody saw her secretly rummage through the trinkets at the bottom of her purse. Hoping ink pen tops would be quarters. Wishing combs with missing teeth to be a dollar. She sucked the wandering finger that had been pierced by an open safety pin posing as a dime. When the plate was passed, the cold metal soothed her warm itching palm.

Nobody saw her wipe the dribble of symbolized blood from the corner of her mouth. The juice, which would have stained her lightly starched blouse went back onto her tongue. The softened cracker was accompanied by the bittersweet fruit of the vine.

Nobody saw her struggle to keep her composure. Shaking hands and hugging familiar strangers. You look nice they told her, complimenting the cream skirt she had soaked the dinginess out of. The scalloped hemline tickled her knees when she stepped forward, walking on swollen feet.

Three days later, yellow tape adorned the perimeter of her front yard. The street and sidewalk were standing room only. The audience was full of observant witnesses ready to give their accounts to those posing questions. In pocket sized notebooks they jotted down words like scream… gunshot…screams… silence… screams. In the midst of all this, her day of glory, nobody saw her.

[i]
 AM

his and hers haikus

his haiku
   His neck is tired
   From carrying all the weight
   Of his heavy mind

her haiku
   She can't pass her past
   And is drowning in regret
   Those tears make deep pools

his haiku
   He has thick skinned feet
   Made to walk bare in summer
   Nothing will change that

her haiku
   She looks in mirrors
   That show things we do not see
   Can she find beauty

[i]
 AM

for mammy and mrs.

Let go and go
Go somewhere
Go anywhere but let go
Be who you are when
you are it
and not
what you are not
when you are not it
If I close my eyes
are you still here
If I cannot hear your words
are you still speaking
If our touch is separated by time and space
Do we still retain the ability to be sensitive
By God's decree
I AM
If you cannot see me, I AM
If you cannot hear me, I AM
If you cannot feel my presence near you, I AM
And defining myself as so
makes it exist
But I still wonder if
I AM one thing, can I still be another
If I AM one place can I still
be somewhere else

We are so dialectic
and diabolical and diaphanous and diabetic
from eating too much candy as kids
instead of the fruits and vegetables our mothers
tried to feed us
And I wish my Mom were here now.
To read my life as I write it.
To thumb through my new dictionary
authored by me
She had a blank book on her nightstand
It longed for the ink that flowed through
her veins
But had to settle for her daily tasks
actions that showed love
but no contentment
Care without passion
Can anyone really be passionate about
mopping a floor
or fixing a lunch for someone else to eat
I mean, it is one thing to enjoy and take pride
in caring for your family
but another for your family
to become you!

in the dark

To stop the pain
Remove the torment
To stop the hate
Cease the hurting
All are in a state of inner confusion
Burning with carnal desires
Don't be embarrassed
I feel it too
In the dark you can touch me
Not seeing my soul
God won't let me burn
if within him I lie
Peace will be found
if for him I live and die
But where do I find comfort here on earth

[i̇]
 AM

little black girl

Don't look down on me
thinking poor little black girl
I AM not poor
Neither am I little
At least not so little that you can
peer down on me with pity
In reality I AM rich
but your eyes are attracted to absence
What you do not see
is everything I have
Things I would share
if your heart were open
But you have obviously
shut me out
in a decision that I have
nothing to offer you

If I look to be in distress
Do not assume that Daddy left
or Mama just lost her job
Matter of fact
Don't assume anything
Don't even look at me
You have no idea what you are seeing
I AM not an angry child

being raised with a chip on my shoulder
I AM not destined to a life of poverty
I have more love in my life than you can imagine
I AM capable of sharing it
But I guess you think my adoration is nasty
Tainted with my blackness
The blackness you fear

Some of you are probably thinking
I'm talking to someone else
You're not racist......
But what was your first thought when you saw me

[i̲ AM]

poetry

You say you don't get poetry
Don't feel the point
Purposeless to you
You say you don't get poetry
Bunch of artsy folk
walkin' barefoot
holdin' hands
while they beat drums
and talk
Revolution
Revolution
Revolution
You say you don't get poetry
Too many vegetarians
who choose not to eat
the meat you long to have
You say you don't get poetry
Too busy scraping
Dimes and dollars
Dimes and dollars
Dimes and dollars
to get enough for just one steak
no no no a chicken breast
or turkey leg
well what about

pigs' feet
Baby
Baby
Baby
You say you don't get poetry
The rhyme the reason
What reason could we possibly
have to spend
time
Wranglin' and manglin'
Wranglin' and manglin'
Wranglin' and manglin'
words
into something hard
to grasp
swallow
and live
You say you don't get poetry
Standing at the bottom of
Maslowe's ladder
waiting for the God's on top to throw
down a little something
Maybe you'll
Catch
Catch
Catch
A scrap

A pair of shoes
Used mop
Empty bag
A book
or Thought
Thought
Thought
You say you don't get poetry
Maybe you will

[i̲ᴀᴍ]

they too will fall

At the break of dawn
We open our eyes
And allow the fears of yesterday to seep through
the small cracks in the floor
Getting out of bed,
Carrying our heavy load
They float down onto the baseboards
Like dried leaves
that have baked in the autumn sun
We step on them
Faintly hearing the snap and crack as we walk
All the programmed mornings have made us deaf to the sounds
To prevent ourselves from
staying in one place too long
We change colors with the leaves
In ignorance, we think we will not drift to the ground
Though that is the very thing that holds us
Going through the day
Among many big trees
We return with more fears
Some repeating themselves
In the morning they too will fall

[I AM]

weapon of mass instruction

I AM a poet
Who sometimes stops on the side of the road
To write down words
Word
I AM a poet
Who may grab a napkin or paper bag or balled up piece of trash
To write down words
Word
I AM a poet
Who pages through dictionaries and thesauruses and encyclopedias
To write down words
Word
I AM a poet
I AM a poet
I AM a poet
and I hold my pen tight
This weapon of mass instruction
Systematic deduction
Be my way of induction into the
Unsung heroes hall of fame
Nobody needs to know my name
I know this work is not done in vain
I AM a poet

I AM Who You Perceive Me to Be

I AM a poet
I AM a poet
Who struggles with the dialectic dialogue in my head
To write down words
Word
I AM a poet
Who has tangled and wrangled and mangled linguistics
To write down words
Word
I AM a poet
I AM a poet
I AM a poet
My hands have been calloused by
The work of my pen
causing friction
from diction
created to crack the encryption
unlocking our minds wisdom
I AM a poet
I AM a poet
I AM a poet
Who works through the Quran,
Bible, Kabbalistic teachings and Gospel of Buddha
To write down words
Word
I AM a poet
Who sometimes forfeits sleep at night

To write down words

Word

I AM a poet

Who discerns between reality and perception

To write down words

Word

I AM a poet

I AM a poet

I AM a poet

Blades and bullets and bombs

Have nothing on the mighty force of my

Pen

Making blood flow into your mind

Stimulating thoughts to help us find

our way through this maze of

socio-political-religious

haze

we call life

I AM a poet

I AM a poet

I AM a poet

[i̇]
 AM

i am half of a relationship

"You cannot belong to anyone else
until you belong to yourself."
– Pearl Bailey

blind faith

During the night
The blind faith of love covers me
Rocking me to sleep
Whispering lies into my ear
The ear you kissed softly
Blowing the breath of life
Heaving my chest
Full of suffocating air
An abrupt stop
Jolts me from my seat
Shocking my peaceful body
Pounding my heart as a drum
Leaving all others
Coming forth unto you
Your light covers my eyes
Unable to see
Your warmth
Curdles my blood
Hugging me
and holding me
Rocking me slowly
In a daze
A trance
A state of intoxication
Floating through the days

Watching as fuzzy dreams fade away
I see your large hands
Coming towards my body
I lay immobilized by fear
Loving the anticipation
You fold me into your pocket
And keep me hidden from hate
Protect me
Hold me
Don't let me go

marvel of the black man

Like a cedar or sycamore
You tower over my mind
The marvel of the black man
can be traced back to the beginning of time
How Eve must have shuddered
each time Adam walked by
If you think she purposely plagued him
Believe me when I say it's a lie
How can you look into the smoldering eyes
And harbor any ill intent
Thank you Lord for men of African descent.
The warm hands caressing destiny
Put me at ease when placed on the small of my back
The black man's ability to stop
and start my world
Is one all others lack
I love my Chinese and Latino brothers
There's nothing wrong with a Swiss or Jew
But when I'm ready to commit my life and love
Only a black man will do.
Maybe it seems that my mind is narrow
And my attractions are coated with color
But it matters not to me what anyone thinks
For my body will never submit to any other
My heart goes out to you with love

And all the understanding society will not give
I know the struggles you face
I know the life you live.
You have been carved with greatness
Your feet firmly placed on the ground
Although you are dealt many injustices
Your strength cannot be brought down.
So do not be fooled by the images you sometimes see on TV
Do not listen to what others say you are
Never allow a person's ignorance to draw from your inner beauty
The frustrations of this world
will not leave your soul with a scar.
You are black and you are beautiful
You are beautiful and you are black
Now let my arms hold your dear body
Let our minds together keep us on track.

[i̇]

untitled and unlimited
(for my unborn child)

Seed has been planted

Life has been slanted

But I understand it

'Cause I AM a woman with a womb

Made to consume

Things in this world

And spit out a righteous child

All the while

She is growing

Knowing what I know

Seeing what I see

An extension of me

Extended from God

Given to the world

[i̇.]

realizations

Reality
   When it is lonely in your arms
   I carry myself to
   Affection
   in my mind
   Just to find a glimpse of love
   Not what you say
   before asking permission to
   enter

Reality
   When your touch is cold
   I nestle deep in my own skin
   and find a warmth within
   my truth
   Because the truth is that
   I AM fulfilling
   My own needs
   While you only fill
   space

[I AM]

postpartum

These blues
These baby blues
been singing to me
Harmonic rhythms in beat
with my thoughts
These blues
These baby blues
got me wrapped around
my Sade CD
Finding ordinary love
In what was supposed to be deluxe
These blues
These baby blues
are wailing out
my name
High and low notes dance
across my range of emotions
These blues
These baby blues
Put me on the floor
in fetal position
Crying salty stories
into the carpet
These blues
These baby blues

got me wondering
if my life insurance policy
is paid up

And there is nothing cute about
baby blues
It is not a pastel time
of
muted
easy to swallow
feelings

These blues
These baby blues
Blues
These baby blues
Baby blues
are rather dark and lonely
Cause everyone else is
Laughing and
Cooing and
Counting fingers and toes
While I count the reasons to
stay alive
These blues
These baby blues
Sent me surfing on

hormonal tsunamis
Hang ten
Can I take five
Maybe pop one or two pills
to help me sleep
These blues
These baby blues
are misunderstood
Understated in books
and talks with family physicians
Worse yet
Forgotten in motherly advice from other mothers
These blues
These baby blues
Aren't blue at all
They are
Invisible

[i̇]_AM

reason, season or lifetime

Are you in my life for a reason, season or lifetime?
I'm not rushing you to stay or go
This is just one of those things I'd like to know
I welcome life's gifts with open arms
But if I peak under the wrapping
Understand, I mean no harm

Are you in my life for a reason, season or lifetime?
Whether your answer be one, two or three
I will not defile our garden of a relationship
By rushing the fruit of our future tree
I do not want to limit our potential growth with labels
But I do find comfort in bonds that are stable

Are you in my life for a reason, season or lifetime?
I'm willing to learn a lesson
A brief encounter will do
I have no fear of commitment
So I ask this question to you

[i̤]

silence
(To Have and to Hold)

We both stand silent with so many things to say
How do we convey emotions and thoughts that have
built walls
Walls that isolate us in our own selves
Selves that cannot stand disappointment one more time
Time that allows the gap to widen between us
Us who lay together but live as strangers
Strangers depending on one another for support
Supporting the idea that we really are alright
Alright to go through the days in a comatose state
State your purpose
(Why are we doing this
Is this what happiness looks like
Do I fulfill you
Do you think you fulfill me)
Can I walk away from this
This image of a love thing
Things don't feel right
Right here is not where I want to be
Be the one to move me
Me the person you once called yours
Yours insinuates ownership
Ownership brings responsibility
Responsibility alludes to commitment

Commitment is that thing we decided not to have
To have and to hold
Hold me, but only in the dark
Darkness covers our deficiencies
(Do you want me
Maybe I still want you
If I didn't I probably wouldn't take the time to
put these wandering thoughts onto paper
I wonder what you are thinking
Should I assume your silence to be indifference
Tell me something
But don't just tell me
Write it down
Put your response on paper
Something I can have and hold)

together

I feel your heartbeat
Next to mine
And I know in this
Moment of time
It is you and me
Me and thee
We two
Together
Forever in this
Moment

unity?

There are babies crying for mothers
   who cannot get past their own tears
   Women hurting for years over the loss of
   what they thought was love
There are children yearning for fathers not around
   Cause they thought they found an easy way out
   feeling trapped by responsibility unplanned
   Not ready to be a man
There are girls in need of women to show them
   what respect looks like
   Only to find ladies diminished by time
   struggling to find respect for themselves
There are boys caught up in confusing noise
   blurred definitions of manhood
   Surely a brother would clear the commotion
   of those misguided notions if only he could
There are young couples trying to survive
   through well intentioned lies
   that mask doubts, fears and infidelity
   Searching for a pair sharing their golden anniversary
A strong example to see
How you and me can make a
WE!

[i̳ AM]

little sister

Looking at me with innocent eyes
Not knowing life is hard
Asking sweet questions
Not knowing you'll have to suffer
Laughing and playing with your friends
Not knowing childhood will soon end
Blowing bubbles and running around
Not knowing you may someday be betrayed
Looking at me with happy eyes
Not knowing

[i．AM]

mama's opus

I want to write a poem for my daughter
She cannot read yet but one day will
has not been formally introduced to poetry
but already understands
I want to write a poem for my daughter
Let the rhythm soothe her mind when it's stormy
Let the repetition wrap her in comfortable consistency
Let the imagery paint pictures behind her eyelids
I want to write a poem for my daughter
Write a poem for my daughter
Because a poem is so intimate and infinite
that it just may do her justice
Write a poem for my daughter
Because I need something to pour the overflow in
Bubbling over…bubbling over
My cup is full and
I want to write a poem for my daughter
It seems so befitting
Me being a poet and all
I mean I should be able to construct an ode
ode to my love
ode to sweet beginning
ode to peaceful purpose
I want to write a poem for my daughter
Give her greater gifts than gold and glory

Leave her a legacy legal documents cannot legitimate
I want to write a poem for my daughter
Ink on paper etched in her memory
of me
Is this a bit too contrived?
Maybe
But we create so many things
Things that sit around with no merit
This poem will have value
If only for she and me, it will live up to its worth
I want to write a poem for my daughter
Write a poem for my daughter
Because that's what writers do
Right?
Write a poem for my daughter
Because that's what writers do
Right?
Right?
Write!

[i̤]

i am what i experience

"If you always do what you always did,
you will always get what you always got."
— Jackie "Moms" Mabley

memories of ecstasy

It's a whisper on my pillow
Echoing lost words of love
Taunting my heart
Teasing my mind
Promises forgotten
Twisted in reality
Intertwined with fear
The trail you left on my skin burns with loneliness
My fingers trace the memory of your body
Bringing back the scent of ecstasy
Uncontrollable reactions
with sensations of peace
I love the moment
But hate the lingering thoughts
It's a whisper on my pillow
Echoing lost words of love
I taste your memory
And lick my lips
The idea of your presence floods my mind
Taboo pictures cradled in emotions
play in my imagination
You cannot conceive what I hold in my heart for you
I busy myself
In an attempt to flee from my thoughts
The twitch returns

Telling me it's been too long
I will not give in to my yearnings
But in the distance I will always hear it
It's a whisper on my pillow
Echoing lost words of love

monotone

You called at least three times last night.
I was nowhere to be found.
Our previous conversations of love and marriage
had never foreshadowed this.
All the pills that culminated into a toxic black substance,
had been pumped out of your body.
You had to be really sore,
because going from life to death
then back to life,
must take its toll.
Your eyes are livid,
without the speck of sunshine they usually hold.
All the machines scare and intrigue me.
The buttons need to be pushed.
In a sick way,
I want to find the one connected to your heart.
Maybe it will shock you,
sending you back to the place you wanted to go.
Would I be doing you a favor?
If you really wanted to stay there,
living would serve as your hell.
I think you need to stay.
Stay with me.
Stay through the fire and brimstone.
Stay through your fears.

Stay for the love you have yet to receive.
The buttons beckon me.
My mind keeps me in place.
An occasional beep sustains my attention,
preventing a deafening hum from overcoming me,
making me into a monotone being.
The lines wavering on the screen
are a signal that you are with me.
Your eyes tell me the lines are wrong.
You breathe and speak.
smile and cry.
What would we be doing if God had chosen for you to die?

mechanically

They entered mechanically
carrying boxes of chicken
with 2 liters of soda tucked under arm.
Heads hung low.
Shoulders curved.
Bodies were draped in dark colors.
Strangers received hugs.
Hands normally avoided
were shaken.
Conversations developed
awkwardly placed between silences
among people who had not seen each other in years.

And this is a tribute to the life of my brother.

[i̲ AM]

rhythm

Drummer Man
Beat me out a tune
Let me feel your rhythm
as we lay under the moon
Reveal life's synchronicities
all in good time
Operate within the cycles
bask in the sublime

Drummer Man
Seduce the skin on your drum
Infuse soul into this pattern
Invoke the holy sound to come
The sanctity of my body is renewed
every time you enter
Your music is to my soul
as repentance is to sinners
Release my body
to these powerful vibrations
Life is honored
through the flow of our libations

Drummer Man
Create the pulse in this heart
Let my reflections of light

accentuate your art
Civilize the uncivilized
with your music we can dance to
Know your position is secure
Because respect is given
where respect is due

Quilting For Life

Bind us together Lord
Bind us together
With thread connecting
our common experiences
and situations
Bind us together Lord
Bind us together
With stitches and knots
that will not be overlooked
Bind us together Lord
Bind us together
mixing color with texture to
Create
Create a palate we can feel
and understand
Tell me a story
to live my life by
Teach me the lesson in peril
They that connect the dots
see the picture
Because we all are connected
Bind us together Lord
Bind us together
With patches that once
covered knees

or dresses hung over a line
to dry
A crisp breeze
Flowing through the trees
Making its way to laundry
that was boiled
and scrubbed
and rung
Now dancing in the moving air
Where do we first hear
that a kiss will make it all right
and if we believe it
is it true
You can smooch
and peck
and kiss
a crying Baby
But it will not chase the chills of a cold night
Love warms the heart
but what about
that drafty wind
that conquers homes built by
love
not cement and strong wood
Bind us together Lord
Bind us together
Cause we've gotten through years on

I AM What I Experience

Massa's fields
but we're
still plowing through the aftermath
we will always recognize
The look the feel of cotton
The fabric of
Our lives are
simply complicated
Inundated with
segregated thoughts
Wants do not coincide
with needs
Heed this warning and learn
to unify your internal Self
Bind us together Lord
Bind us together

[i̱ AM]

history-whostory

The rivers of life flow through my eyes
Treasures of the world sprang from my thighs
Mathematics and medicine were conceived in my cheek
After I spit them out, I tried to civilize the Greek
The history of life can be read on my back
Knowledge of self sits in my lap
My toes are painted with science and philosophy
Wars have been waged and fought all because of me
My body is divided into many lands and territories
They all reflect life's full glory
My fingers are outlines of the Creator's dream
My babies suckle the finest creme
All people want pieces of my skin
And though they believe they have conquered
They have never even been in

your presence and absence

You came inside
And left something behind
A memento
souvenir
a keepsake
Something worth keeping
Maybe
Left there to grow
manifest
emerge
possibly
A reminder of your presence
Or absence
The missing piece
To my heart
A bridge
To you
An unstable connection
Shaking with fear
confusion
pain
And it grows
Bringing thoughts never thought of
Feelings never felt
Tears never cried

And an un-heard-of amount of joy
One that could never be received
Or conceived through any other means
A confirmation of life
Certificate of completion
And it cries
Revealing hunger
a need to be loved
cared for
understood
And it cries
cries
and cries
Until it stops
And is heard no more
And so it dies
Drowning in the tears never wiped away
The saltiness of it all
Burning the flesh
Leaving scars
Spots that never truly heal
Places that tell a story of
Your presence
Or absence

[i/AM]

i saw a man cry

I saw a man *cry* last night
silent overflow
from the flood in his mind
I saw a *man* cry last night
Gentle masculinity marking
salty trails down his cheek
I saw *a* man cry last night
The sole survivor of emotional confrontation
among the dead sea
I *saw* a man cry last night
Facing forward with no
fear of being seen
I saw a man cry last night
Making me rethink my thoughts of manhood
and raise the pedestal higher
I saw a man cry *last night*
and I recognized this old friend for the first time.

[i̤]

morning drink

I smiled
all day
long
Remembering the way
You put
your cream
in my
Coffee

just dessert

I AM ready for life
Life that flows freely from fallopian tubes
I AM ready for giant steps
Giant steps that stretch the tight place
between my thigh and crotch
I AM ready for air
Air that burns my nose a bit but settles in my
lungs like it's meant to be there
and fresh thoughts
Thoughts that have not been in my mind
long enough to become stagnant and stiff
I AM ready for the rainbow
Rainbow of colors encompassing every
mood I can have, have had, and will have
I AM ready to rise in love
because falling hurts
to rise in love
because heights are unlimited whereas
depths have bottoms
to rise in love
because we fall down but we get up
hopefully
I AM ready for abundance
Abundance that runs through my pores like sweat
from a hot night with you

and for feelings
Feelings that take over and lead my body
to where I need to be
I AM ready for poetry
Poetry that reads to the rhythm of my scattered life
I AM ready for the seeds I have scattered to blossom
Bloom into scarlet red flowers
Those with letters on their foreheads know what I mean
I AM ready to stop erasing and start embracing
to be touched
Touched with fingers that reach through my soul
and feel the warmth of my light
More importantly, I AM ready for my light
Blind me
I AM ready to walk blindly into the day
I AM ready to live
I AM ready to die
I AM ready to have the whole piece of cake
and still see it in its full glory
Yes I think I will have cake
Calories and all
I will have my cake and eat it too
Because I AM ready
I AM ready to be full

[i]

i am my thoughts

"In the province of the mind,
what one believes to be true either is true
or becomes true."
– John Lilly

evolution

How do we walk upright
carrying the weight
of
Life
and
Death
with such a thin line between the two
Recognizing how fast
we can cross from
one
side
to
the other

[¡AM]

the self in me

There is a love that envelopes me
Cradling my heart in the warmest folds of passion
I speak of a love that dances in my mind
It is a touch like a sweet promise
One not yet spoken
But heard by my ears
A whispering wind that chills my soul
A thickening plot waiting to unfold
A tender vision soon to appear
A fleeting dream coming near
My heart's desire
Anticipations fire
A righteous love
Flying down like a dove
Bringing peace
And I stand still
The movement around me dizzies my thoughts
I'm not sure that I want to think
If cognition brings doubt
Keep it away
Away from my love
My life
My peace
My piece
…of hope

Faith keeps this in the wind
Where it cannot be tainted
Or painted the color of fear
So I hold this near
Or it holds me
Drawing truth and clarity
Bringing my Self out of me.

stuttering strength

I AM strong
Standing tall
For all to see
An image of perseverance
And beauty
Yes I AM single
Yes I AM black
Yes I AM a mother
Yes money is something I lack
But don't you see this smile
The way my cheekbones rise
The high steps my feet take
The proclamations of joy my mouth makes
The posture with which I walk
The love I infuse in my talk
Oh I AM strong
If that's what I need to be
To keep the breath in me
For my eyes to open and
see another day
A way to survive through the lies
betrayal
and rejection
Defend myself from life's insurrection
Injections of peace from the books I read

Planting seeds in my mind
Telling me thoughts behind
everyone's little deeds
Explanations of broken
men and women
Livin' day to day
in a way
That breaks another's peace
Specifically mine
In a day and time when I need the love of another
to fortify my weak spots
Blot the tears of yesterday
and now
How can any of us do this by ourselves
The shelves in our dark closets are full of
cruel offenses
that have weakened our
defenses
to the point that one
look
word
question or
touch
Hurts
So sensitive to the world that
I cannot even try
to be me

I AM My Thoughts

And let people see
the truth of my fragility
Fragile
in the most dangerous form
I look so normal
and happy
and free
from the noose of my memory
What you see is not what you get
But most haven't figured it out yet
And we thought
black women
did not ponder
suicide
I
AM
strong

[i̱]

for us by us

The revolution is now
Change has come
In you and me
We are getting it on
Task
Bask in the beauty of
our own abilities
And it's phat baby
With a 'ph' like the farm
We mean no harm
But it's time we take over
And over and over
We've been dealt the blows
of social injustice
and economic homicide
Or political ambush
with traces of spiritual rape
And it is true
all of it
believe that
But this is phat
with a 'ph' like the farm
We mean no harm
But it's time we take over
Because no one is going to do it for us

Get to the back of the bus
and shut up
they said
And we did
Every time we bought Tommy Hilfiger
We did
When we allowed Clarence Thomas
to be appointed
We did
Each yes m'am and no sir
We did
The songs we blasted on our stereos
that fed our minds inferiority
We did
But no more
We holler at the top of our lungs
And it's phat baby
With a 'ph' like the farm
We mean no harm
But it's time we take over
For us by us we say
But this time the words are more than a logo
that we sell to a larger
richer
whiter
company
This is

For us
By us
In us
And it's built up strong from the bottom of us
Cause now the brothers smile at me on the street
then ask how are you today sister
And they really want to know
Not one of those polite greetings that is given
no thought
This is Black Thought
Because as much as we recognize our individuality
we are the same in so many ways
The family tree started from one seed
So it may branch out spanning
Accra or Mbeya
to Tennessee or Virginia
or Paris and Istanbul
but the seed is the same
And this is phat baby
With a 'ph' like the farm
We mean no harm
But it's time we take over
We mean no harm
On second thought
Maybe we do
Get what's coming to you
And to get it

It has to get got from someone
This might be fun
Reparations…Reparations…Reparations
Reparations can't even pay your bill
It has piled up so high
There are not enough mules and acres
to take care of this
I have been compounding interest daily
The Senate Committee says they
will meet on the issue
That is fine
But in the mean time
We're making this phat baby
With a 'ph' like the farm
We mean no harm
But we are taking over
…our lives

choice words

And let us not grow fat
from our own words
Words we are forced to eat
Words that become
hard to swallow
after they pass our lips

for sisters sonia and nikki

I AM a woman who has kicked down doors
Free my wings and watch me soar
More than a womb added to a man
Shaped this divinity out of sand
With power to create
So call me earth
Bless this existence
Each time I give birth
Release love and peace
from between my thighs
Find God's truth deep in my eyes.

understanding maslowe

I AM
Climbing
higher
and higher
Up the hierarchy of needs
So I need more from you
or maybe less
Because I AM giving more to myself

headlines

Extra
Extra
Read all about it
The information superhighway
is full of
Webmasters
with whips and chains
ready to bind our minds
Don't leave your papers
behind

creationism

If we were made in his image
are we not Creators?
Creating our thoughts
Creating our deeds
Creating our aspirations
Creating our needs
Creating our friends
Creating our foes
Creating our loves
Creating our woes
If we were made in his image
are we not Creators?

peace like a river

Whatever my lot though has taught me to say it is well, it is well with my _ _ _ _

Some of the greatest gifts
I ever received
Came cloaked in what
I perceived as failure
Pain and
Punishment
But that ain't irony
That is life
and my inability to see
What is truly out there
for me
My greatest obstacles are
My Self,
Attraction to wealth
Choices that lead to bad health
and always wanting something else
When was the last time
I sat back and said
It is well
It is well
It is well with my soul
Hold all the past hurts in and
they will overcome you

We've got to release
Teach each other and ourselves how to relax
Stacks of bills
Stacks of dirty clothes
Stacks of fears
and wasted years
Pile up on the mind and
Compress the time
Into one
big
unhappy life
Why even bother
Going to work everyday
for pay that
ain't sufficient
And I AM not talking dollars
When did we decide that expensive
clothes and cars can fulfill us
We are living in a drought
Doubt the person inside and
You are gone
Letting commercials live your life
Letting bushels cover your light
No
We quietly whisper inside
Because we're trying to travel
to that place where we can say

It is well
It is well
It is well with my soul
Unfold the fortune in that cookie and
find some peace of mind
'Cause Confucius says
Don't worry
Be happy
Or maybe that was
Bobby McFerrin
But the message is still true
Do you know where you're going to
Do you like the things
that life is showing you
Us is a mahogany people
Mixtures of red, black and brown
Up and down
Killer and clown
Going round and round to nowhere
Walking on treadmills but never traveling
Sweating with no fruit to show
for our labor
It's quitting time y'all
Because we need to sit back on our porches in
rocking chairs and hum
It is well
It is well

It is well with my soul
Cold summer days can confuse the mind
They say we're getting close to the end of time
Better get right church and let's go home
Which ain't as easy as clicking two red shoes
Whose idea was this anyway
From peace
To watery womb
To drama filled life
To dark tomb
and then back to peace
I would have rather stayed there
In the first place
Races are for rats
I want us to walk across
The finish line together,
Hold up our blue ribbons
and exclaim
It is well
It is well
It is well with my soul
And we will hold each other
in deep embraces
feeling our hearts beat
to the rhythm of
It is well
It is well

It is well with my soul
And we will in unison say
It is well
It is well
It is well with my soul
And I can see this vision for all of us because
It is well
It is well
It is well with my soul

[i̱]

Letter From the Author

July 17, 2002

Dear Friend,

What can I tell you in this letter that I have not told you in the pages of poetry you just read? These pieces reflect passages found in many people's diaries and daily journals. Is it alright to talk about depression? Do people want to hear of my battle with intimate relationships? Do any of us still care about the socio-economic ills plaguing our society? Can I spark a discussion on suicide? Are we intrigued by a story of personal growth and self-love? I hope so.

A lot of us are emotionally constipated. (Yes, I said what you think I said.) We hold things in. We cover our hurting hearts with painted on smiles. We numb ourselves with food, sex, insignificant others, money and all the things that leave us wanting. What does it take to release the things we do not want in our lives and have the courage to retain the happiness we were created to live?

For me, poetry has served as a powerful release, an opportunity to view myself clearly on the page and make changes accordingly. The collection of poems you just read chronicle some of these changes.

Letter From the Author

I see poetry as an avenue of communication and connection. It is not the rigid memorizations and interpretations we had to do in structured classrooms. It is the feeling you get when a cool rhythm makes you nod your head. It is the tightness in your stomach as you see yourself in all your naked beauty and gruesomeness. Poetry is the clever way we live our lives given stringent limitations such as having only 26 letters in the alphabet to make the words to express our wide range of experiences!

Thank you for traveling with me. I hope the trip you took through my thoughts, experiences and relationships made you smile, think and be inspired.

Have confidence in yourself. You are a child of God, made in His/Her image. Why ever question that or hold such a holy position in low esteem?

Guard Your Spirit and Mind!

Stephanie

Acknowledgements

Thank you to my family. My foundation is strong because of you. Daddy, your support and belief in my endeavors is a great comfort when the world feels cold. Mama, I know what kind of woman I want to be because I have always had you as an example. Christy, me and you us never part… makidada…me and you us have one heart…makidada. I love and like you. Nia, thank you for coming into my life. I love you so much I won't try to put it into words. I'll live my whole life acting it out! I am thankful for the poets who have come before me as teachers and way-makers: Nikki Giovanni, June Jordan, Sonia Sanchez, Amiri Baraka, Gwendolyn Brooks, Countee Cullen, Langston Hughes, Maya Angelou and countless others. To my confidant and fellow writer, Keisha D. thank you for your help, support and listening ear. Thank you Shannon for the beautiful book design and layout. Maybe one day I'll have the money to properly pay you. Thank you Jaquessa, Myra, Carly, Patrice, Alimah, Caye, Danielle, Chandra, and all the women who make me proud to have this much estrogen inside of me. To the men who have played important roles in my life: Brian, Tarik, BA, Stephan, Derrick, I am thankful for the experiences.

   Lord guide me, keep me humble and on purpose.
     Thank you for this and so much more. Amen

We want to hear from you!

Please share your thoughts and opinions about this book. Go to www.InfotainmentTandP.com. You can give us feedback about I AM, order books for friends and family and get information about other talented artists and their products.

Please send me _____ copies of Stephanie Pruitt's I AM: A Poetic Journey Towards Self Definition. I am including $9.95 plus $3.50 shipping and handling per book. (check or money order)

Name: _____

Address: _____

City: _____

State: _____ Zip Code: _____

E-mail: _____ Phone: _____

Mail this order form to:
Infotainment Talent and Publishing
Attn: Order Fulfillment
1708 21st Avenue South, Suite #149
Nashville, TN 37212

(please allow 2-3 weeks for delivery)